Straight A's In Schools

Ain't No Joke

Inspiring Academic Excellence In An Unforgiving World

REPORT CARD	
Reading	A+
Writing	A+
Mathematics	A+
Science	A+
History	A+
Art	A+
P.E.	A+

KEITH G WRIGHT

KEITH G WRIGHT

Straight A's In Schools

Ain't No Joke

Straight A's In Schools

"Ain't No Joke"

Inspiring Academic Excellence

In An Unforgiving World

By

Keith G. Wright

Ain't No Joke Books

MIAMI SHORES, FLORIDA

www.AintNoJoke.com

Straight A's In Schools Ain't No Joke:
Inspiring Academic Excellence, In an Unforgiving World.

Copyright © 2006, 2015, 2017, 2018 by Keith G. Wright

Manufactured in the United States of America

For information address:
Keith G. Wright
Ain't No Joke Books, Inc.
Miami Shores, Florida 33150
www.AintNoJoke.com

Straight A's In Schools Ain't No Joke 2020
ISBN-13: 978-0-9778342-1-1
ISBN-10: 0-9778342-1-2

Keith G. Wright
www.AintNoJoke.com

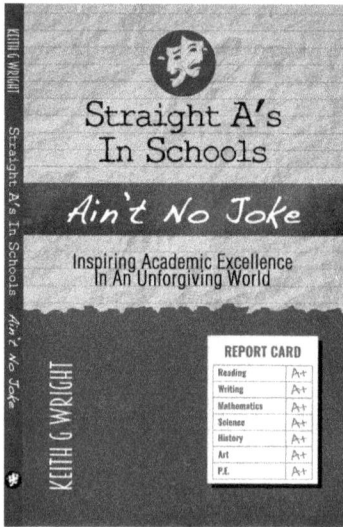

STRAIGHT A'S NO JOKE CONTENTS

Introduction

My experience with academic excellence began early in my childhood, having been raised by a school teacher mother, who drilled the importance of academics, highlighted one day by her announcement at the beginning of my 4th grade year, as she said, **"Don't bring no C's in my house!"**

I had never gotten a C before, and didn't think too much of her statement at the time, so I simply filed it in the back of my 4th grade consciousness. It wasn't until 2 years later, in the 6th grade, that I found out just how serious my mother was about "them C's."

Growing up, my mother encouraged me to play just about every sport - football, basketball, baseball, soccer, volleyball, track and wrestling. But during the baseball season, as a 6th grader, at Old Orchard School in Toledo Ohio, my mother pulled me off the baseball team, because I got a "C" - one "C" - on my report card. I was a very good player, and was having a dominate breakout season. So, it was no surprise that my baseball coach would be a little concerned about losing one of his best players.

But let me tell you, I was also a little concerned about my baseball coach's mental health, when he showed up at my house one day to speak to my mom about my playing status. Now understand, I'd been living with this lady all of my 6th grade life, and even I was shocked that she pulled me off the team for getting a "C"... but I would not have been shocked if my baseball coach didn't make it out of my house alive. Well, because the conversation between my mom and the coach was deemed "adult talk", I never knew what was said between them, but I did know that Keith G. Wright **still wasn't playing any more baseball** that year.

Certainly today, that would be unheard of, almost incomprehensible, to think of a child being pulled off a sports team because of one "C" grade. But here's the thing my mom knew that nobody else knew or even thought about... and here's the thing that made her a wonderful mother.

My mother knew I was a better student than what I was displaying. My mother knew that she couldn't afford for me to drift into mediocrity and risk becoming comfortable and complacent with that. My mother knew that the message needed to be sent early... that my academic standards would remain high, regardless of what activities I became involved in. And she knew I would buckle down and return to achieving those standards of only A's & B's... and I did.

And my mother knew, as a single parent, that she and she alone was responsible for my success as a student and as a young man. She did not bend under the pressure of me wanting to play little league baseball. She knew that no one else was really concerned about me and my future. Ultimately, I knew and appreciated that she was the one person guiding me, in the classroom, on the playing fields, and in life. She was the one person pushing me to excellence.

Over the years, since that fateful 6th grade moment, I've never brought another 'C' in to her home... and over the years, I've realized it wasn't hard at all to achieve & maintain academic excellence. Doing so is really about your priorities, about what's important to you, about your own goals and dreams... academic excellence has always been about, what you really want in life and what you're willing to sacrifice for it. And that's the essence of what this book is all about... outlining and laying out the steps to consistently make straight A's in school, and inspiring amazing youth like you, to take action toward your unlimited future. Achieving perfect grades is all in your hands and all in your control. Simply decide this is what you want... and the steps are easy, so let's GO !

S E C T I O N

O N E

ACCEPT THE
Straight A's
CHALLENGE
&
ACADEMIC
EXCELLENCE

No Joke Academic Axiom #101: Accept The Straight-A Challenge. The most ambitious students challenge themselves to achieve academic excellence. They challenge themselves to achieve perfect grades for at least one school term. Challenge yourself... take one term, one quarter, one semester, whatever your school calls it, and commit yourself to straight A's. Challenge yourself to do whatever it takes, sacrificing everything, for just one term out of your school career, at least once out of the 12 years of school, to get nothing but straight-A's. For one term in your school career, commit yourself to education, knowledge, and your future. Watch the enormous feelings of confidence, pride and satisfaction swell up within you, when you commit yourself and achieve excellence.

For the rest of your life, you can live with the satisfaction that you had a perfect report card. I'll bet the feeling is addictive and I'll bet you'll never want to settle for less for the rest of your life. Keep a copy of that perfect report card to show it off to your parents, your future children, and grandchildren, **as a symbol of what powerful young people can do when they apply themselves.** If you haven't already, get your taste of perfection while you're still young... while you can. Challenge yourself today, right now, to academic excellence. **Do you accept the challenge ?**

ACCEPT THE CHALLENGE

If you've never had straight A's before, or even if you struggle with getting passing grades in school, you may harbor an inner belief that there's no way you're ever gonna get straight A's in school... you may be feeling a bit intimidated or anxious, thinking about the hard work and long hours of study involved to get perfect grades... maybe that little voice of negativity in your head is all you hear.

But I'm here to tell you, **there's a bigger voice, in your heart, that says yes you can... and yes you must !**

Listen ... I've been where you are, and I came to realize that this world and this life ain't joking with young people. There are so many obstacles that trip us, so many barriers that imprison us, and so many rules, laws and traditions that intimidate us. Living and succeeding in this world is difficult, intentionally, by design seemingly, that very, very few people ever understand it or find their place in it. Mediocrity and failure are everywhere.

MEDIOCRITY AND FAILURE? .... OH, THAT'S NOT FOR YOU !

As the next generation to lead this world, **your life is invaluable, and your life is filled with great ambitions and promise...** throughout this journey of academic excellence, you will overcome many obstacles and bring forth the greatness of your own individual human spirit, to accomplish all that your heart, mind and soul can envision !

No Joke Academic Axiom #102: Wise students recognize the hard work you already do, and make small changes in daily habits which yield big results to academic progress.

Give yourself credit, and think about the work you put in everyday, just getting to school. Listen, listen … if you're attending school everyday, then you're already doing the hard part… **the rest is simple small habit changes and mindset.**

Think about all the things you do in a typical school day. You wake up early in the morning, stumble to the bathroom, brush your teeth, wash your face, take a shower, get some breakfast if you have time, gather your book bag, and walk to the bus stop, stand and wait for the bus, in all kinds of weather.

When the bus arrives, you're pushed and mushed, as everyone crowds the door, then you try to find a seat, with a bunch of sweaty, smelly kids, packed tightly in seats like a can of sardines… enduring stop, after stop, after stop, as more kids board the bus… until you finally get to the school campus and exit the bus… **and you still haven't even gone to your first class yet.**

After you exit the bus, maybe you catch a breather to stretch your legs, and talk with your friends for a bit, before the first bell rings… and then it's class after class after class after class, as you sit for hours at a time, lesson after lesson after lesson… when lunch break comes, you have to rush through your food, but sometimes the lunch lines are so long, you don't get a chance to eat… if you take a P.E./ Gym class, you often have no time to shower or clean up afterwards, before rushing off to your next class.

You attend every class until the school day is over, but maybe you have an extracurricular or after-school activity you participate in, such as sports, cheerleading, dance, student clubs, or tutoring even... after those activities are over, it's time to wait on the bus again, get pushed and mushed as you board the bus, find a seat with other kids packed like a can of tuna this time, because these kids are really smelly after a full day of school and activities... and football players smell the worse after practice, right?

Finally, you make it home, to do chores, eat dinner, shower, and finish homework and study before getting to bed at a decent time to get enough quality sleep... just to wake up the next morning and start the whole thing all over again. **Give yourself credit !** What you do everyday is hard work, and can be quite stressful... I've been there too.

GIVE YOURSELF CREDIT

Listen, listen ...you're already working hard just to show up everyday, but what if I told you that **if you simply change a few habits during the course of your day**, that you'll be well on your way to academic excellence? What if I told you, that **if you redirect some of that hard work and energy,** that you could get closer and closer each day toward consistently achieving straight A's? **Well, I'm here to tell you, and show you, just how possible your goals and dreams can be !**

AIN'T NO JOKE ACADEMIC AXIOM #103:

EMBRACE

The Urgency Of Now

I believe your life and your future ain't no joke... but your urgent attention and preparation to your future is paramount right now. If life was a video game, life has stacked the game in such a way, that the first 18 levels (years) of your life, are the absolute most important.

If you master these 0 to 18 levels, then you get the keys to the next higher level... which provides enormous benefits and privileges, starting with High School Graduation, the pride of parents and family, multiple college acceptance letters, college scholarships, corporate internships, paid job offers, mentorships from highly acclaimed professionals, opportunities to study abroad and travel all around the world... and a very bright future, with many options and choices.

If you fail this level, 0 to 18, then you get automatically pushed to a lower level. Unfortunately, there are no do-overs, no take-backs, no repeating nothing... at 18, they automatically push you out to your appropriate level, based on your actions and play at previous levels 0 to 18.

Getting pushed to the lower levels doesn't mean guaranteed failure in life, as you can always come back from behind, through the power of your own human spirit... but, it does mean enduring a tougher road, with less support and fewer resources... it does mean you pay for everything you want and need, including paying for your own college education, and it does mean you probably have to work a lot harder, and keep your emotions in check, through the inevitable frustrations, as you struggle & strive your way back to the next level.

No Joke Academic Axiom #103: Embrace The Urgency Of Now, the importance of 0 to 18, and its impact on the next level of life.

EMBRACE THE URGENCY

This level you're on right now, 0 to 18, is to be taken very serious... make the most of this time in your life, this time to prepare, to learn, to grow, to develop, to set goals, to dream big dreams, and to build a remarkable life for yourself... master this level, and then level UP !

Think about it, there's been millions of kids before you, who have gone through elementary, middle, and high school... and there will be millions of kids after you, who will go through these same levels. Everyone gets the same 24hours /7days /365 days a year, and everyone gets their 18 childhood years... but now it's your time, and your turn... you simply have to accept the challenge, and you simply have to decide, right now, today, to get what's yours... and simply decide, to be GREAT in this world.

Top Strategies To Straight A's & Academic Excellence

DO NOW

1) Accept The Challenge

 - You deserve academic excellence, accept it !

2) Give Yourself Credit

 - Recognize the hard work you currently do

 - Make small changes that lead to big results

3) Change Your Mindset

 - Understand purpose & importance of 0 to 18

 - Get serious & make the most of your teen years

4) Embrace The Urgency

 - A childhood is a very short time to prepare for real life

 - This is your time, your turn, take action now !

S E C T I O N

T W O

BUILD YOUR

Personal Brand

OF

EXCELLENCE !

Gather 'round me youngsta's, for 'um bout to tell ya' the ole tale of the teen who never studied, who never cracked open a book, and still got straight-A's… Uh, Not!

One of the biggest peer pressure fables known to teenagers, and all of mankind, is the kid who brags about getting all A's on his report card, without ever studying. How many times have you heard that one? Hey, talk about peer pressure. That will certainly get you feeling depressed and inadequate real quick.

But I'm here to tell you, don't buy into the notion that your peers are getting straight-A's and barely studying. I'd be a rich man, if I had a nickel for every teen that told me they had a 3.8 GPA and they "really don't study at all". Nobody is born an expert in algebra, chemistry, and history.

These are things you have to learn and you have to study. But what I can tell you is there's definitely one thing that can help teens study less and still get good grades.

No Joke Academic Axiom #201: Wise students have figured out that the best approach to getting good grades is to get as much knowledge as possible "during class" time. They learn as much as they can "during class". They stay focused "during class", and ask many questions. They treat the classroom as a sacred place of knowledge & learning.

These students pay attention during class when the knowledge is coming directly "from the horses mouth", if you know what I mean. Then they walk out of the classroom with a solid understanding of the course material, much more so than the poor schmuck who was goofing off or daydreaming during the entire class. For the wise teens, by the time they get home, it's just a matter of repetition, studying for reinforcement, and getting prepared for the tests... they don't have to work nearly as hard as the guy whose head was wandering around the room and later is totally lost with his homework.

But any kid who tells you he just kind of "shows up" and get A's, isn't being 100% truthful with you, and that's because of the peer pressure that *they* are feeling. Be slow to believe everything your friends brag about, especially when it comes to them *not studying* and still getting excellent grades.

Time and time again, teenagers tell this old "not studying" fable just to fool their peers into not studying... it's a trick., I tell ya'. There's a lot of teens running around the schools, getting good grades, and pretending they don't study at all. They lead weak-minded students into skipping class, and goofing off, while they, instead, pay attention and study diligently... these same kids go home and study twice as much as you do, because they know how important education is, and they have parents who will certainly remind them. But hey, if they really told the truth, they wouldn't feel so cool.

Listen, listen ... when I was in middle school and high school, all of my friends, and even my very best friends, knew they couldn't talk to me in a classroom. My friends could talk to me about anything, before school, after school, on the school bus, before class, after class, in the hallways, in the cafeteria, in the courtyard, in the bathroom, and in the library even... but one place, even my best friend knew he couldn't talk to me... was in a classroom.

The classroom was a sacred place of learning and knowledge for me... it was my time to work toward everything I hoped my life to be... it was my time to learn about this world, my time to stretch my mind... it was my time to compete and show I was capable of being an excellent student... it was my time to practice discipline in preparation for more difficulties to come... it was my time to respect teachers who provided valuable wisdom & knowledge to better my own life, today & tomorrow... it was my time to build myself to the student and person I wanted to be... it was my time to relax, quiet my mind, calm my energies, and meditate on learning... the classroom was peace for me.

SACRED CLASSROOM

Listen... I didn't care what all the other students were doing, but even my best friends knew what time it was when I walked into a classroom... and they respected it.

This leads us to **No Joke Academic Axiom #202: Strategic students know that there's a time and place for everything**. They understand that a childhood is a short time, and four years of high school can come and go in a blink of an eye. Because of this, the wise teenagers know to play when it's time to play. They study when it's time to study. They listen respectfully to their teachers while in the classroom, and they listen to their music players outside of the classroom. The wisest teens focus on what's most important at that moment. **They enjoy the company of their friends when it's time to be social, and they quietly concentrate on the lessons at hand, in any learning environment.**

TIME & PLACE FOR EVERYTHING

Ask yourself what is the number one reason that you go to school. Then school is the time and place to focus on that number one reason. **Paying attention in class actually makes your homework go a lot easier. Not paying attention in class makes your homework a big mystery and misery.** Ask yourself, what's the number one reason you practice your favorite sport, instrument and other activities. Then practice is the time and place to concentrate on that number one reason. Ask yourself, what's the number one reason you take out the trash, wash the dishes and clean your room. Even while doing the household chores, it's important to focus on that number one reason. Hey, if you're washing dishes and you're not paying attention to what you're doing, those dishes might not get as clean as they should be. Would eating off of dirty dishes be a problem? You Betcha'! There's a time and place for everything, and the wisest and most successful teenagers understand it.

Build Your Personal Brand

Branding is so important to business owners, digital entrepreneurs, and influencers... but the classroom is also a space where you can start to build your personal brand... the classroom is an extension of who you are and what you represent... the teacher is your client, who demands a quality product or service, and rewards you with grades, feedback, recommendations letters, mentorships, and critical insight for you to continue to build your very successful personal brand and business.

BUILD YOUR PERSONAL BRAND

No Joke Academic Axiom #203: Savvy students start early to build their personal brands, in and out of the classroom. Everywhere you go, especially in the classroom, start building your personal brand… its your image, your company, the assignments you turn in…. your work ethic, focus, attention to detail, how you dress and present yourself, your communication skills, and how you respond in challenging & adverse situations. Build your brand today, for the future you desire & deserve.

Draw The Line - Disrespecting Teachers

You already know how much I respect & appreciate teachers, and I'm here to tell you, that if you're serious about academic excellence, you're gonna need to draw the line on some things within the classroom… **if you're serious about accomplishing anything major in life, then you're gonna have to start drawing lines, on what you will or won't do, in order to protect your dreams.**

Let's start by drawing the line, right now, right here, where you sit reading this book - in a classroom, with a teacher.

No Joke Academic Axiom # 204 : Scholarly students draw the line on disrespecting teachers… they understand the immense value & knowledge that teachers bring to their lives & future, and they know the history of oppression all over the world, where ruthless dictators banned people from being educated... **never disregard or disrespect anyone providing an education to you.**

Draw the line on arguing with a teacher for correcting your actions, when you know teachers represent education, knowledge, and a brighter future for you, when you understand your important purpose for being in school, and certainly, when you know you're wrong, ... why take it out on a teacher, when you're the one who's late to class, you're the one who's out of dress code, you're the one with no assignments completed, no class supplies to even attempt to work, when the teacher is simply doing his/her job to push you to greater heights ...and, more importantly, when you know and fully understand the power and value of education to fuel your own dreams and ambitions... what's the point of your disrespect? Please draw the line on disrespecting teachers.

Ask yourself, why would anyone disrespect a person dedicated to helping you improve your life? Teachers should be the first people high on your list to garner your respect everyday... teachers, substitute teachers, assistant teachers, teacher aides, and even student teachers... everybody deserves to be respected, especially the teachers & school staff helping you everyday.

NO DISRESPECT

There was a time in history when many people were banned from getting an education. Because of the importance of knowledge and the power of education, there are still many people, even today, who would prefer you stay dumb and ignorant... but not teachers.

If education is power, and knowledge is love... then teachers show students love everyday by imparting valuable knowledge and building a powerfully educated student... a student who can then go out in this world, to do anything, become anything, accomplish anything, travel anywhere, and conquer all your dreams.

No Joke Academic Axiom # 205 : No Joke students never run from knowledge, and they never disrespect a teacher, viewing teachers like parents away from home, who care enough to hold you to high expectations... understanding the sacrifice teachers make everyday, to provide valuable knowledge, and teach powerful concepts, which can carry you a lifetime... draw the line on disrespecting teachers.

Draw The Line - Skipping Classes

Ask yourself, what happens when you regularly skip class? You might fall behind academically, you develop hard-to-break bad habits, you get used to not going to class... and when you do finally go back to class, you feel lost, frustrated that you've fallen so far behind, depressed & angry... possibly becoming a class disruption, possibly getting referrals, and suspensions, leading to more missed classes, falling behind even further, with more bad grades, and more frustrations... geez, man, just draw the line on skipping !

Isn't it better to attend class and learn even if just one thing, than to skip and learn nothing at all? Why come to school and walk around all day, or hide out in the bathroom, or hide out in substitute classrooms ... what's the point of skipping - when you have EVERY night off to go home, every weekend off, every Xmas off, every Thanksgiving off, every school holiday, every teacher workday, every spring break, every summer break, even bad weather/storm days off ... after all the time off you're given, why still come to school and SKIP ? **...ask yourself, where do you draw the line on skipping classes?**

NO SKIPPING

No Joke Academic Axiom # 206 : The smartest students draw the line on skipping classes, realizing the classroom is a sacred safe place of learning. Beyond a requirement for graduation, it's the classroom routines & environment, that provides the discipline and structure to prepare students for ultimate successes in their future life, preparing for success in the real world. Smart teens have figured out that while in the classroom, you are away from the other skippers, away from the negative influences, away from the drama, away from the altercations, away from hard-to-break bad habits... **draw the line on skipping classes.**

Top Strategies To Straight A's & Academic Excellence

DO NOW

1) Treat The Classroom As Sacred

- Get maximum knowledge within the classroom
- Do not tolerate or accept distractions from friends

2) Understand Time & Place For Everything

- Focus on what's important at that moment
- Study when it's time to study, play when it's time to play

3) Build Your Personal Brand In The Classroom

- Your behavior and quality of work represents you
- Develop your work ethic, focus, and attention to detail
- Your brand matters to your image, company, and future success

4) Draw The Line - Disrespecting Teachers

- Display upmost respect for teachers
- Accept the love of knowledge & the power of education

5) Draw The Line - Skipping Class

- Show up everyday for your own future
- Make the classroom your safe space for learning & support

S E C T I O N

THREE

DAILY
Reading
&
PERSONAL GROWTH

Daily Reading Ignites Academic Excellence

"...BUT WHEN BOOKS ARE OPENED, YOU DISCOVER YOU HAVE WINGS."
- Helen Hayes

If you've read about leaders in history, or studied world history, you probably know that from ancient times to even now, the first thing any ruthless dictator wants to do is outlaw reading and education amongst the common citizens, to fulfill his dominant control and reign of terror. Many tyrants throughout history have run a campaign of "oppression through ignorance", in an attempt to keep "the people" from any claims of equality, civil rights & liberties, and any sense of empowerment within their own countries. The outlawing of reading and education is scattered densely throughout the world's history. We saw it happen in China, in Afghanistan, in Nazi Germany, and even here in America during the slavery era. Why would so many leaders of men try to keep you from reading and learning new things? Because, it's the one thing, reading, that ultimately frees you, frees you from the shackles of oppression. It's the one thing that gives flight to your dreams.

Yet this is the one thing you can control, for your life. It's the single most important act you can control in your life, to read and become educated, which gives you an undeniable force of power. From now on, whenever you see a book, any book, think of the many leaders in history, the many agencies, the many corporations, the many politicians, and the many forces in this world and this life, that would want to keep you from truth and knowledge... forever ignorant. **From now on, when you see a book, think of that young slave, hiding in a dim lit corner, stealing away precious moments of reading... stealing away precious**

moments of freedom. Thirst for books, thirst for knowledge, and thirst for reading. Your life depends on it.

The year 2019 marked the 65th anniversary of a Supreme Court ruling granting equal access to education, for all American citizens. But ask yourself, w**hy would anyone not want everyone to be educated?** Because education is power, a life-long-lasting, from-one-generation-to-the-next, power. Because an educated person can compete in this world. Because an educated person is not easily misled. Because an educated person has their destiny in their own hands. Because an educated person is not intimidated by fancy words, contracts and unconstitutional laws, and other games that powerful people play. Get your education. Empower yourselves and take control of your lives. Make this world and this life what you want it to be... not what someone else thinks you only deserve.

DAILY READING

No Joke Academic Axiom #301: Daily Reading is the single most important life building activity you can possibly do. Reading gives your dreams the freedom to soar through the universe. I am so convinced of its power and influence on your success, that it's the one thing I wish all children would adopt. There is no real success without reading. It is a simple reality of life. You will see this truth eventually. **Either adopt the habits of expanding your mind through reading now, or later experience the unfulfilled potential of what your life could have been.** At some point, everyone understands the power and benefits of reading, even if it's much later in their adult life. And everyone, at some point, wishes they could have done more as teenagers. But guess what? You're still young enough to get it now. You're still young enough to become passionate about reading and education.

Benefits Of Daily Reading Toward Straight A's

1) Reading Improves Vocabulary & Expands Word Knowledge
2) Reading Builds Stronger Analytical Thinking Skills
3) Reading Improves Memory, Focus, and Concentration
4) Reading Enhances CREATIVITY & mental FLEXIBILITY.
5) Reading Boosts Writing & Language Skills
6) Reading Ignites Innovation & Progressive Ideas
7) Reading Enhances Empathy & Cultural Awareness
8) Reading Reduces Stress and Increases Tranquility
9) Reading Opens Windows & Portals to Other Dimensions
10) Reading Gives Flight To All The Dreams In Your Heart !

You're still young enough to incorporate reading into your daily activities. Some kids figure this out early in life, and they have a decided advantage in all they embark on, owning a developed mind, strengthened by worldly exposure, reinforced by historical reference, and nourished by vital knowledge. Bill Gates got it early. Oprah Winfrey got it early. The truly great ones got it early, and so can you.

Every person on the face of this earth has something uniquely wonderful to offer the world. Every person has at least one great idea within them to make our lives better, one great song, one great book, one great invention, and one great way to change the world. Early in your lives, become insatiable readers, expand your mind, and demand more out of life. Reading will take you places you may never have the opportunity to go, and reading will take you to places you may never want to go. Educate yourself through consistent daily reading. Life is short; get serious about reading.

Bookstore One-Page Reading Activity

By the time you've finished reading this book, my hopes are that you'll walk into any bookstore and immediately feel like a kid in a candy shop, spending literally hours sampling books like chocolates, reading, browsing, thinking, reflecting, and having your mind stretched and strengthened.

No Joke Academic Axion #302 : Practice the weekly bookstore reading activity of visiting any of the large bookstores, like Barnes & Noble, slowly circle around the bookstore, visiting each section, scan the books in that area, then grab one that catches your eye... read the cover, read the back, skim through the tables of contents, find any section of that book which interests you, then read just one page... **that's it - just one page**... return the book to the shelf, and move to a totally different subject/topic section.

Maybe "start-up" in the Business section, scanning books on small business development, giant fortune 500 corporations, real estate investing, or entrepreneurship legends... you might be inspired to start a business while you're young, building your own brand of business success... all it takes is reading one page.

Flow into the Computers & Technology book section, and take a "byte" out of the pages of artificial intelligence, autonomous navigation, robotics, and 5G technologies… you might be inspired to develop an idea to positively impact our future human experience with these controversial technologies… it takes just one page.

Pour into Cooking, Food, & Nutrition book section… and baste in the healing power of the selection, preparation, and cooking of fresh, organic, nutritious foods… it may inspire you to blend new recipes, and transform your own health, mind, body, and soul, through zestful cooking and healthy eating … just one page.

Drift into the Automobiles, Aircraft, and Transportation book section… and take a spin in the latest automobile designs, aircraft engine and powerplant technologies…you might be inspired to create an ingenious safety gadget for programmable & self driven cars… reading just one page.

Travel over to the World History book section… take an enlightened look into the Ancient, Middle Ages, and Modern eras, and investigate cultural events in real hidden history… you may be inspired through understanding past history, to make a better future for the next generations…. sometimes it takes just one page.

In this activity, it isn't necessary to read the entire book, simply taste a sample of each book, feed your many interests, and take a bite sized morsel from the brightest pages… by skimming books, flipping pages, skipping ahead, jumping back, flowing through the contents until you see something that sparks your attention, then drill down further for deeper knowledge and inspiration. Allow your mind to roam free and do what it does best... allow your mind to wander through the possibilities of this world, this life, and the positive impact you may contribute to it all.

BOOKSTORE READING ACTIVITY

Do this activity once a week, and I promise you that, one day, you'll walk out of that bookstore a different person... with an insatiable appetite for books, literature, information, and knowledge of all kinds... **and I promise you, it will ignite your school studies, grades, and overall academic performance, in & out of every learning environment... all it takes is just one page at a time.**

Draw The Line : Mobile Phone Addictions

Over the years, we've been told that technology exists to better our lives, to make our lives easier, they say... but please be slow & careful, to quickly adopting everything new into the core of your lives. Some technologies are simply driven by dollars... created by money grubbing people, who will stop at nothing, to make more money, at your expense, even it means using harmful psychological technologies to capture the attention of the masses.

Have you ever heard of the term, "Nomophobia"? It is a combination of the three words "no, mobile and phobia", defined as a fear of being without your phone. It's what happens when you travel out of a coverage area with no cell towers and no cell signal. It's what happens when your battery runs out, and you're scrambling, frantically finding an outlet or a power cord to borrow. It's what happens when you're in class and the teachers asks you to put your phones away, or better yet, when the teacher takes your phone to keep until the end of class. It's the anxiety and despair your feel… over a being without your phone.

According to research, many people now are sleeping with the cell phones, showering with their cell phones, consumed by fear of being without a mobile device. Many students would rather face school suspension than to give up their phones temporarily to a teacher, who is simply trying to keep them focused on education. Research suggests the average person spends nearly 4 years looking down at a cell phone… looking down, while walking, looking down, while talking, looking down, while driving, looking down, while eating, looking down, while sitting, looking down, in classrooms across the nation, looking down at your phones… **plugged in and tuned out, unable to pull away, addicted and controlled by the manufacturer, who intentionally designed everything about the phone, to keep you mentally and emotionally obsessed and fixated on your phone… controlled like a puppet on a string.**

"LIFE BEGINS AT THE END OF YOUR COMFORT ZONE."
- Neale Donald Walsch

Just a few minutes checking your phones at night may disrupt sleep patterns for hours afterwards, decrease focus capability, leading to hidden stress, sudden aggravation and quick tempered reactions.

NOMOPHOBIA

No Joke Academic Axiom # 313 : Courageous students are not willing to be controlled & manipulated by mobile technologies, grasping the importance of focus in the classroom, realizing the power of human touch, personal conversation, real friendships, and genuine human interactions. They don't bury their self worth in selfies, likes, followers, or online friends they've never met or will never talk to... instead, their self esteem comes with living a life without limits, without boundaries, without artificial controls, without living like a puppet on a string... **where do you draw the line on mobile phone addictions?**

Top Strategies To Straight A's & Academic Excellence

DO NOW

1) **No Joke Academic Axiom #301: Daily Reading** will ignite academic excellence, and is the single most important life building activity you can possibly do. Reading gives your dreams the freedom to soar through the universe.

2) **No Joke Academic Axion #302 : Practice the weekly activity of visiting any of the large bookstores, like Barnes & Noble, slowly circle around the bookstore, visiting each section, scan the books in that area, then grab one that catches your eye...** read the cover, read the back, skim through the tables of contents, find any section of that book which interests you, then read just one page... that's it - just one page... return the book to the shelf, and move to the next section.

3) **No Joke Academic Axiom # 303 : No Nomophobia -
Courageous students are not willing to be controlled & manipulated by mobile technologies...** recognize the importance of focus in the classroom, and realize the power of human touch, personal conversation, real friendships, and genuine human interactions.

SECTION

FOUR

THE

SPIRIT OF

Competition

The Lessons Within The Spirit Of Competition ...

When I was young, I noticed that the children around me all had different talents. They seemed to all have their own set of skills that made them better than the next person at certain things. This can be intimidating for many teenagers, as they constantly compare themselves to their peers. **But don't worry; we all have our own abilities that make us unique and good at something. And you have yours as well.**

Some kids were good students, and seemed smarter than the rest. But it didn't mean that no one else got A's and B's on their report cards. Some kids were better athletes, and seemed naturally gifted on the playing fields. But it didn't mean that no one else played on the sports teams. Some kids were just prettier and more handsome, it seemed. But that didn't mean no one else had girlfriends or boyfriends. Just think about it. Have you ever seen a gorgeous man or woman, with an average looking guy or gal? You can win at life, even though someone else may seem better at a certain thing. You can win at life when you develop your ability to compete.

Have you ever played a game with friends or family in the swimming pool, to see who could hold their breadth the longest under water ? And if someone beat you the first time, you wanted a do-over, to try again and again, until you held your breadth the longest... until you won. That's the true essence of competition... That's the same determination and competition you need to bring to the classroom.... just because someone is getting A's and you're not, only means you should make positive changes, and try again and again, just like in the swimming pool.

We must learn to compete in the classroom, and in every aspect of life, to not believe or concede we can't do a thing... because you can do anything, when you put your mind to it, when you try again and again, when you never ever give up... when you compete !

COMPETE IN THE CLASSROOM

Yes, a competitive spirit can defeat superior talent any day of the week. Regardless of what skills and talents you have or don't have, you can still pull yourself equal with, or even ahead of, the next guy.

If you desire to succeed, and are willing to do the things necessary to compensate for your lack thereof, then there's nothing in life you cannot do. Learn to improve yourself where you are weak. Learn to make yourself better. Learn to compete!

The principles of competition are not only important in sports, but are indeed most important in real life. Think about it; isn't the game scoreboard a lot like a school report card? A report card is an indication of how well you are doing in the classroom. The game scoreboard is an indication of how well you're doing in the game.

Think about all the dreams you have for your life, and all the adventures you want to experience in this world. Then take a good look at your life right now. Are you on track to where you want to be in the future? Are you winning or are you losing? If you're barely on track, you might get a C-grade for a tie score. Are you winning big? If so, you get an A-grade. Are you losing? D-grade.

Are you really far behind in achieving your goals? Are you losing by a lot? F-grade. Remember, you don't play sports in school just to possibly make it to the professional league. You play sports to learn how to compete, to compete in life. Sports programs help students develop a competitive spirit. It helps students gain skills that will help them compete in the world. In sports, you learn how to set goals for your team, to prepare for your opponent, to work hard, to play fair, to make adjustments when you're not playing well, and to come from behind when you're losing. In sports you learn how to do what you have to do… to win!

No Joke Academic Axiom #401: Compete To Be Your Best - always look in the mirror for the answers in your life, challenge yourself to be a better person everyday, and develop your ability to compete… compete in & out of the classroom, and compete in every aspect of life to bring out your very best.

It boggles my mind that so many gifted athletes can compete on the fields, the courts and the arenas, but can't compete in the classroom. They lift heavy weights, run for miles, and practice for hours, yet won't grind the same, in the classroom. They won't put in the same level of competitiveness in their education. Why? Ask yourself, are you winning at life? Are you competing in the classroom… are you a champion of your own real life?

Everybody has something, and everybody is lacking something. It doesn't matter what it is for you. It matters most that you compete, that you develop your skills and talents, and that you work to get better at the things you may lack. It matters most that you take the steps and do the things to keep you "in the game".

42

Compete In The Classroom - Participation

Classroom participation is probably one of the most under rated aspects of learning, yet it may be the easiest thing to do. You don't have to be the smartest student in the room to participate... you don't have to be a straight-A student to participate... all you need to do is show effort, show you care about the subject, you care about learning, and you care about getting the best possible grade... classroom participation isn't hard at all, but it will help you significantly, in ways you might not understand.

PARTICIPATE IN LEARNING

While some teachers offer additional credit and grades for class participation, it's always good to be active in the learning process, by asking questions and offering ideas, which is known to help students obtain & retain vital information, while enhancing understanding, clarity, and knowledge of the subject.

No Joke Academic Axiom #402: Compete in the classroom through class participation; simple yet effective effort... participation increases retention of vital information, while enhancing engagement, understanding, clarity, and knowledge of the subject.

Class participation is also a way for teachers to know that you care about learning and you're putting forth visible effort towards improving as a student. In the end, through class participation, you'll become a more engaged and confident student... and confidence is everything in life. The more you participate in the classroom and are actively engaged in the subject, the more you'l remember, the easier your homework will be, and the better you'll score on tests and quizzes... and all it takes is simple effort on your part.

Compete in The Classroom - Assignments

If you analyze your syllabus, you'll probably notice a lot of points toward your final grade which are attributed to homework, projects, class participation, and extra credit... often times these things may contribute at least 50% to 80% of your final grade... truthfully, these are all effort grades, and everyone has the ability to show effort. Ask yourself what grade should you always get on homework? what grade should you always get on projects? what grade should you always get on extra credit?

No Joke Academic Axiom #403: Compete in the classroom through simple yet effective effort at home... have the mindset to always score 100% on homework, projects, extra credit, or anything you are able to take home and complete... 100% on everything done at home, 100% of the time... no excuses.

100% ON ALL HOMEWORK

I'm here to tell you, with the resources students have now, with the adults at home who can help you, with the other students you can collaborate with, and with all the technology at your disposal... **there is no reason to ever get less than 100% on homework, projects, extra credit, or anything you are able to take home and complete**... 100% on everything done at home, 100% of the time... it's simply no excuse.

Compete in The Classroom - Learning For Understanding

You've probably heard the phrase that "knowledge is something nobody can ever take away from you," which underscores the power of education, learning, and knowledge. Think about this… how is it, that a wealthy person can lose all his/her money, then rebuild and make it all back again? Because they have knowledge and understanding, which is something they can never lose, even as all the material valuables are being taken away.

No Joke Academic Axiom #404: Compete in the classroom through simple effort, seeking clarity and understanding of the subject… study to learn & understand, not simply to memorize. Knowledge is something nobody can ever take away from you. Memorization is short and fleeting… yet, education, knowledge and understanding, are forever.

Compete in The Classroom -
… Study Anywhere, Everywhere, Anytime

For the busiest teens, study time can be a rare commodity, especially when you're over obligated with a high level of extracurricular activities … finding time for quality & effective study isn't easy with everything you have going on in your life.

No Joke Academic Axiom #405: On those days when a long block of study time isn't available, you simply have to chip away the valuable study time, by seeking to study anywhere, everywhere, anytime.

STUDY ANYWHERE, EVERYWHERE, ANYTIME

Keep your book bag with you at all times, filled with school books, notes, and assignments. Study every chance you get, everywhere you go... study while you're en route to anywhere, on the bus, on the train, riding in the car, on the airplane... review your notes while you're waiting on anything, waiting at the bus stop, waiting in doctors/dentists office, at the laundromat, in the airport terminal... study in school, in the courtyard, in the cafeteria, in the library, in the gym, on the stadium bleachers, in an empty classroom... study in nature, in the park, under a shaded tree, by the lake, by the beach... study while you're going out, at the museum, in the mall, at the bookstore, at a fast food joint, at the coffee shop, on a college campus... study at home, at the kitchen table, in your backyard, by the pool, on your balcony, even in the bathroom. Waste no idle time... be prepared and ready, to study anywhere, everywhere, anytime.

Top Strategies To Straight A's & Academic Excellence

DO NOW

1) No Joke Academic Axiom #401: Always look in the mirror for the answers in your life, challenge yourself to be a better person everyday, and develop your ability to compete... compete in & out of the classroom, and compete in every aspect of life, to bring out your very best.

2) No Joke Academic Axiom #402: Compete in the classroom through class participation; simple yet effective effort... which increases retention of vital information, while enhancing engagement, understanding, clarity, and knowledge of the subject.

3) No Joke Academic Axiom #403: Compete in the classroom through effective effort at home... have the mindset to always score **100% on homework**, projects, extra credit, or anything you are able to take home and complete... **100% on everything** done at home, **100% of the time**... no excuses.

4) No Joke Academic Axiom #404: Compete in the classroom through seeking clarity and understanding of the subject... study to learn and to understand, not to memorize. Knowledge is something nobody can ever take away from you. Memorization is short and fleeting... yet, education, knowledge and understanding, are forever.

5) No Joke Academic Axiom #405: On those days when a long block of study time isn't available... you simply have to chip away the valuable study time, by seeking to study anywhere, everywhere, anytime.

SECTION

FIVE

THE
IMPORTANT
Intangibles

Intangibles - Diminish The Drama

One common trait of most straight-A students I've met through my many years of working in schools, is their ability to diminish or dismiss drama. Let's face it, drama and conflict seem to be everywhere in our schools... I get it, some kids are just aggravating, right?... it's practically a daily occurrence for an argument or a fight to break out in some schools. But nothing good happens when students are involved in alterations or embroiled in drama... referrals happen, suspensions and school absences happens... missed classes, missed tests, quizzes, and missed assignments happen... falling behind and frustration happens... but with drama & conflict, straight-A's don't happen. If you're gonna be serious about academic excellence, it will be important to develop conflict resolution and deescalation skills to help diminish & dismiss the drama, in order to create a calm and peaceful school environment, and make certain you stay in school and stay focused.

No Joke Academic Axiom #501: Diminish & Dismiss The Drama ...enlightened students draw the line to diminish and dismiss drama in schools, by practicing Restorative Justice, conflict resolution, and deescalation strategies... to create a calm, peaceful, and productive learning environment for everyone... no drama, no altercations, no absences, no suspensions, no digging holes, no burning bridges, no disappointments, no setbacks.

DIMINISH THE DRAMA

Draw the line on petty, silly, garbage disagreements, which eventually escalate into harmful & hurtful incidents you'll later regret. Draw the line on confrontation, and "he-say, she-say, but-nobody-said-it-to-you" drama.

Draw the line on boy-likes-another-girl, so I'm-gonna-fight-the-other-girl silliness...nothing lasts forever, relationships end, and people move on ... it's just something we have to learn to deal with.

Draw the line on physical violence to resolve any disagreements and differences... we are not animals in the wild jungle... we are blessed with a brain, heart, communication skills, and a desire to become better, for a bright future ahead.

Draw the line on having a victim mindset - everything that happens to us, isn't always driven by some outside force, beyond our control... often the problems we face in life, we bring on ourselves, and have the power to change. Draw the line on allowing negative people and negative influences to impact your thinking & your emotions, in your daily life.

Intangibles - Restorative Circles

If you've never experienced the power of Restorative Justice Circles, please ask your teacher, counselor, or administrator about the Restorative Circle process, which is a method of addressing broken relationships, and the many things that go wrong in our schools... a process of actions, activities, and dialogue, which serve to address harmful or damaging behaviors, while bringing together all affected people, to discuss, respond, and repair the harm done to individuals and community. It's also a process of allowing people to be heard without prejudice, to express thoughts without limits, and allowing people to admit a wrong, take responsibility, and apologize, without judgement... Restorative Circles allow students to enter the circle with a concerned voice, respectfully listening and responding to each other, in their own truth, and leave the circle with resolution and a peaceful spirit.

RESTORATIVE CIRCLES

Intangibles - Build Relationships

It's easy for us to recognize the fact that we all have strengths & weaknesses, in everything we do, certainly in schools... but by collaborating and working with other students who also strive for academic excellence, students can help each other through their strengths, and learn from each other to improve on their academic weaknesses.

No Joke Academic Axiom #502: The smartest scholars collaborate with like minded classmates, to assist each other through their strengths, and improve on their weaknesses.... in each class, they make a friend - have a friend - be a friend - help a friend - keep a friend... a strong intangible toward academic excellence.

Collaborating with a classmate who is ambitious and motivated to get good grades, will serve to keep both of you accountable and motivated, providing a needed push and support. If you're absent from class, you'll check on each other and fill in the important blanks of what you've missed… keeping in mind, when absent from school, it's your responsibility to find out what you missed and complete what assignments are due.

MAKE A FRIEND IN EVERY CLASS

Intangibles - Easy A's, Low Hanging Fruit

Always capture the "low hanging fruit" in school, with straight-A's… these classes include Art, Music, Drama/Theatre, Home Economics, Life Skills, and P.E./Gym class, or similar classes, which often aren't demanding or difficult… for assignments, this also includes homework, quizzes, take home projects, and extra credit for each class… maintain expectations and appropriate effort to gain straight-A's in the "low hanging fruit" classes & easy assignments.

No Joke Academic Axiom #503: Savvy students never miss an easy A opportunity, in easy classes. Resist the egotistical traps of not dressing out in P.E./Gym class, not rehearsing in Theatre, not painting in Art, not practicing an instrument in Music, and not making a donut in Home Economics… draw the line on getting F's in easy-A classes, the easiest classes in school, throwing away an easy 'A' which could help your GPA, for graduation, college entrance, and scholarships… **easy A's get you closer to straight-A's.**

ALWAYS GET THE EASY A'S

Intangibles - Get To Know Your Teachers

Getting to know your teachers may be one of the most important intangibles toward getting the best grades possible. It doesn't mean being the teacher's pet or being a "brown-noser"... **it simply means realizing your teacher is human, and so are you...** while understanding your teacher's overall expectations, their likes and dislikes, and their view of a model student.

In the same way that athletes allow sports coaches to be tough, to be vocal, and to be demanding, allow your teachers to set high expectations, and demand the best of you... allow your teachers to be quirky and hold a weird set of rules & standards... and allow yourself to be coached by teachers, to learn from each teacher, and to take that knowledge and those experiences into your future success. Like sports coaches, when you like, respect, and trust your teachers, you'll automatically work harder and hold yourself accountable as an excellent student... when you take the time to get to know your teachers, you open the windows to true academic excellence.

GET TO KNOW YOUR TEACHERS

Key strategies to getting to know your teacher include:

a) **Attend class** - greet teachers with a warm smile and positive attitude... never absent and never late... you'd be surprised how much test information is covered during class. Some teachers may go over entire exams & test materials during class... teachers recognize your good attendance as a student who cares about learning. Teachers view your tardiness as lack of respect for the classroom and instruction time... students arriving late lead to constant disruptions in learning.

b) **Sit in the front of class** - even if a teacher has a predetermined seating chart, it won't hurt to ask to sit in front. Sitting in front of class makes it easier to focus and engage with the tempo & information flow of the classroom... sitting up front, with less distractions, it signals to other students you're serious about the classroom & learning... and signals to teachers that you're present & ready.

c) **Participate in class** - ask questions, as they say, no question is a dumb question... and challenge new information presented with your previous learning... being an active participant in your own learning simply ignites more learning and retention, making homework and tests easier...even small things like volunteering to assist class by handing out or collecting papers and materials, gets your body moving and encourages engagement.

d) **Stay humble and polite** - your teachers are human, and so are you... be respectful & attentive, show interest and value in your teachers' educational expectations & vision... be willing to share your own future education goals and vision... teachers often make the best mentors, and can assist you with recommendation letters, scholarships, valuable advice & encouragement, and help steer you on the right path, toward graduation, college, and career. Always address your teachers with their appropriate title and last name... show respect for everyone and try to maintain the same zest for knowledge with all of your teachers... for you, straight-

A's aren't a one time deal, it's a lifestyle and a continual journey toward life-long learning and excellence.

e) **Ask for help - ask how you can become a better student** - ask questions - ask for advice - ask for teacher expectations - ask for alternative study resources and materials - politely speak up and let the teachers know you are serious about your education. Just remember, many of your teachers dreamed of becoming a teacher, and have always wanted to be in a position to help the next generations... they want nothing more than to see you succeed in a very big way !

Intangibles - Student Grade App

Over the many years working in schools, I've come across some of the best students, and some of the worst. Believe it or not, I've met a student who spent an entire 9th grade year receiving a 0.0 GPA... not a 2.5, not a 1.5, not even a 0.5... nope, I'm talking about a big double-0, a 0.0 gpa. Ofcourse I had many questions for this student, like "how do you come to school everyday for an entire year, and end up with no credits, nada, zilch?"

On the other hand, I've met many straight-A students, at various middle schools and high schools, and ofcourse my #1 question was, "how do you get straight-A's in every class, in every term, for the whole school year?" Interestingly, what I found as the most common answer & common behaviors of straight-A students, is the daily checking of their school district's grading App. Every school district has a website/App where students can track their grades, assignments, exams, and overall academic progress. Some of the

56

widely used grading programs include PowerSchool, Blackboard, Moodle, Edmodo, Progress, Infinite Campus, Skyward, and Google Classroom. In my local school district it's called Edline.

CHECK GRADE APPS

During my first conversation with 11th grade student Ariel, I noticed she had straight-A's in every class since her 9th grade year. When I asked her how she does it, without hesitation, she said, "Mr. Wright, I check Edline all the time, everyday... like some kids check Facebook, I check Edline... like some kids check Instagram, I check Edline... in the same way these kids check social media, I'm checking my Edline... Don't get me wrong, I check my Facebook & Instagram too, but I ALWAYS check my Edline... I check Edline at least 3 times a day, and some days I check it before every class, just to see how I'm doing or what I might have missed... so I don't miss anything!"

No Joke Academic Axiom #505: Tenacious Scholars are driving toward straight A's, utilizing student grade apps daily, and recognize you can't improve a thing, if you don't check a thing !

Another straight-A student, who was in the 9th grade at the time, answered the question quite frankly, as if I should've already knew the answer... she said, "I check Edline constantly, Mr. Wright... well, how can you improve on something, if you're not checking on it - Duh ?!"

Well, I guess they answered my question... now, I'm not saying you should obsess over checking your grades & academic progress like these students, but given a choice, you might want to obsess watching over your own real life progress, rather than obsess watching over somebody else's fake life on social media.

Intangibles - Organized Personal Growth

It's not enough to say get organized, set a daily schedule, and improve your time management skills…. true, all these things are important, but one of the biggest lessons I've learned in life, is "don't overindulge on the sweets of life, when you haven't done the meat & potatoes of life." In other words, everyday of your life, set aside time for you, time to work on your own personal growth… work on becoming better everyday, moving you closer each day toward your goals & dreams.

PERSONAL GROWTH HOMEWORK

Specifically, how does that look? Set aside a block of at least 2 hours everyday for your homework and studies, everyday, 7 days a week. Inevitably, there will be days when you don't have homework to complete… but you still use that block of time to work on you. No homework? … work on your weaknesses. No English homework? … work on your writing skills, paragraph building, and sentence structure. No Math homework? … work on your quadratic equations and polynomial factoring. No Science homework? … work on total understanding of the periodic table and the process of balancing chemical equations. No homework at all? … work on building your vocabulary, work on learning a foreign language, work on developing that business start-up idea you have, work on researching colleges & career options and understand how those decisions may impact your future.

No homework? ... read a great self-help book, to help you make the changes you know you need to make, have a lengthy conversation with your mentor, study the factors which build resilience, and work on the things you struggle with. **Regardless of whether a teacher gives you an assignment or not, don't allow that to determine whether you put in work or not. Each day of life, maintain the mindset of personal growth, self improvement, and maximizing your own 24 / 7 / 365** ... resist the television, resist the video games, resist the mobile phones - it's all a trap, anyway, to keep you from growing, developing, and preparing yourself for an amazing future !

Intangibles - Win The Day

It's understandable that you can get overwhelmed at times, with all the assignments, readings, research papers, projects, exams, quizzes, and oh, can't forget those states standardized testings... but I want you to approach it, one day at a time.... **I want you to quiet your mind, calm your heart, and win this day ! Do whatever is required of this day, and understand you have everything you need, already inside you, to overcome today's obstacles, and run with perfection today.**

WIN THE DAY

Today, attend every class, on time... today, greet your teacher with respect and a smile... **today,** sit in front of class, participate, and stay engaged... **today,** take notes and write down every assignment and due date you've been given... **today,** avoid the drama when you start hearing the gossip & rumors, refusing to contribute to it, and refocusing on what today means to you... **today,** check your student grade app, several times... **today,** set aside a block of time for personal growth... **today,** attach your plans, goals, and dreams with every action you take... ask yourself, if what you're doing today, will help you reach your plans, goals, and dreams of your future. Win today, and build strength and momentum for tomorrow! **Win today, each day, one day at a time, and the greatest future you can possibly dream of, is right there in the palm of your hand - GRAB IT NOW !!!**

Top Strategies To Straight A's & Academic Excellence

DO NOW

1) **Intangibles - Diminish and dismiss the drama in schools, by practicing Restorative Justice, conflict resolution, and deescalation strategies.**

2) **Intangibles - Collaborate with like minded classmates, to assist each other through their strengths, and improve on their weaknesses....** in each class, they make a friend - have a friend - be a friend - keep a friend... a strong intangible toward academic excellence.

3) **Intangibles - Never miss an easy-A opportunity.** Resist the traps of not dressing out in P.E./Gym class, not rehearsing in Theatre, not painting in Art, not practicing an instrument in Music, and not making a donut in home economics.

4) **Intangibles - Student Grade App :** Utilize student grade apps daily, and recognize you can't improve a thing, if you don't check a thing !

5) Intangibles - Organized Personal Growth

Set aside a block of time everyday for your homework, studies, improving weaknesses, planning your future, and personal growth., everyday whether you're assigned homework or not.

6) Intangibles - Win The Day

Approach straight-A's one day at a time & win each day… quiet your mind, calm your heart, and do whatever is required of this day… **WIN THE DAY !**

S E C T I O N

SIX

ONLINE
INDEPENDENT
LEARNING

LEVEL UP

No Joke Academic Axiom # 601 : Life will always try to trip & trap you into mistakes and failure... but you are born for this - built for this - unstoppable in all you decide to pursue... so make the online journey your great pursuit, and accomplish all the goals and dreams in your heart !

The year 2020 has ushered in an epic crisis, impacting every citizen throughout the world. The Coronavirus presents a challenge unseen by most people living today, yet it is a challenge we must meet head-on, overcome, and conquer.

One of the biggest impacts on students has been many school districts' decision to implement an online school program, in the name of student & family safety. Whether you like or dislike the prospects of online school, I want you to know something... I want you to understand there's a bright side to all of this... a silver lining underneath the dark cover.

"WHEN THE WORLD GIVES YOU LEMONS, MAKE THE SWEETEST LEMONADE..."

As the next great generation of young future leaders, you were born into immense technology, and you're comfortable and savvy enough to turn these difficult times into a most positive experience. It's time to show the world who you are, what you're capable of, and showcase your abilities to adapt and thrive against any challenges thrown your way. Simply, it's time to make that sweet lemonade out of the sour lemons the world has given you. I want you to know that you can, and you will, succeed in the online school environment.

The following pages are critical strategies that will help you flourish during your online learning and take control of your own educational development and destiny. Life will always try to trip & trap you into mistakes and failure... but you will adjust, regroup, and navigate through all the shenanigans. Why? Because you are a leader and you take ownership in your own learning. Because you are curious about the world and question the status quo. Because you are an independent thinker, and have your own unique set of passions and interests. Because you are determined to succeed, and will push through the most difficult challenges. Because you possess the personal will power and motivation to be consistent in your work and studies. Because you have access to the resources and support to achieve your goals, and you know how to reach the right people whenever you need individual help & clarification. Simply put, you are born for this - built for this - unstoppable in all you decide to pursue... so make this online journey your great pursuit, and accomplish all the goals and dreams in your heart !

"IF YOU'RE NOT WILLING TO LEARN,

NO ONE CAN HELP YOU...

IF YOU'RE DETERMINED TO LEARN,

NO ONE CAN STOP YOU !"

DISTRACTION & PROCRASTINATION ARE SIBLINGS OF SELF-SABOTAGE

No Joke Academic Axiom # 611: Distraction & procrastination are siblings of self-sabotage... don't sabotage yourself. Self discipline to avoid procrastination & distraction, is simply another way to show the world who you are, and what you're made of.

After working in middle and high schools for over a decade, and talking to thousands of students over the years, at some point I began to realize the deep problems students suffer with distraction & procrastination... if I didn't understand it before, I certainly get it now... as one student tearfully admitted to me, "Mr. Wright, you just don't understand how hard this is, I don't know how to fix this procrastination, it's a real problem."

Distractions and procrastination have been problematic for many generations, for both teens and adults alike... even more sinister is the fact you now have to work/study from home in an online environment. While working from home, here are two main areas of distractions which lead to procrastination, and strategies to overcome them.

NEVER LET ANYONE OR ANYTHING DISTRACT YOU FROM NOTICING HOW AMAZING YOU ARE !

Family Distractions : Although we love our family members, it's critical that they understand the importance of your study time, and respect your designated workspace. It may take longer for younger siblings to adjust, but with consistent conversation and positive affirmations, everyone will be on board to helping you strive toward straight-A's, by limiting interruptions. Have a family conversation letting everyone know your desire for academic excellence, ask for help and accept family support, and appreciate even the smallest gestures of support... then whenever family members see you sitting behind your desk, they will immediately understand and respect your work-study time. Like a classroom, you too should treat this area as a sacred place of knowledge and learning... no playing, no eating, no sleeping, just like the classroom. Embrace the fact that your family members will now encourage you to make positive study choices and hold you accountable for academic success.

DISTRACTION WASTES OUR ENERGY, CONCENTRATION RESTORES IT !

Electronic Devices / Internet / TV : Let's just be honest here... watching movies while studying simply doesn't work... constant phone calls, texts from friends, and social media alerts are just as damaging to your effective study. You can't do several things at once and do them well. Eliminate the television completely, and reduce the music to low background volume if you must listen. Move your phone far away from you, and consider placing your phone on silent or airplane mode, to eliminate texts and alerts. Contemplate using an automatic away-text-message to inform your friends you are studying and will answer their calls/texts on your study breaks. Same for internet use on computers - turn off wifi to build a barrier from quick web surfing. When the weather is comfortable, do take advantage of outdoor spaces to get some sunlight, fresh air, and be further away from common distractions inside the home... patios, balconies, lawn chairs, pool decks, or under a shaded tree.

"MANY A FALSE STEP WAS MADE, BY STANDING STILL"

However challenging things may seem, remember you are built for this... yes managing the onslaught of family, friends, electronics devices, and general noise around a busy house can be very difficult, it's true... and having the discipline to eliminate distractions of phones, television, and music, is not an easy task by any means. But this is what you're capable of doing, this is what you must do... and this challenge is merely a prelude to the many more difficulties which lay ahead in adulthood. Don't sabotage yourself. This is where the lights come on and true stars step onto the stage and perform. This is where you show your abilities. During these most challenging times, this is where you prove your inner drive and ambition. Self discipline is simply another way to show the world who you are and what you're made of. Hey, it's all just a dress rehearsal for adult life, the wonderful future you've chosen for yourself.... so perform well, my friends... perform well !

CREATE A WORKSPACE INSPIRED BY YOUR GOALS, DREAMS, AND THE LIFE YOU ULTIMATELY WANT TO LIVE

No Joke Academic Axiom # 623 : Create a workspace, inspired by your goals & dreams, and driven by the life you ultimately want to live... your workspace is where dreams are built, brick by brick, day by day... it can be anything you determine... but it must be inspirational if nothing at all.

Your workspace is more than proper lighting, comfortable seating, and a few essential supplies... **your workspace is where dreams are built, brick by brick, day by day.** Although most of us are limited to certain areas within our homes for a workspace, most likely it will be your bedroom. Wherever you choose, it's important to have a dedicated space that's quiet, clean, and personalized for you. Once you've decided on a location, consider these factors for success:

Remove Distractions: Remember there's a time & place for everything, and your work/study area is the time and place to increase your focus, and challenge your mind. Remove the distractions of phones, video games, social media sites, and any interruptions.

Access To Supplies/Resources: Before you start working, you'll need to have easy access to all necessary supplies and every resource required to work efficiently.... avoid getting up & down to constantly retrieve basic things. Consider having a calendar nearby and a writing/stick board for your to-do lists.

Be Inspired: Your work area doesn't have to be cramped and stuffy... it can be anything you determine. **But it must be inspirational if nothing at**

all. Design your study area to mirror your personality and enhance your goals. Place motivational quotes and inspiring posters in this area, along with personal photos of special family members who motivate you to achieve, and role models who encourage you to be your best. Consider building a vision board, symbolizing all of your goals, dreams, and future accomplishments. Your workspace should be about maximum productivity, and a reminder of why you do this work everyday, in the first place... a daily reminder to strive toward the amazing life you ultimately want to live.

COMMUNICATION & COLLABORATION ARE PILLARS OF ONLINE SUCCESS

No Joke Academic Axiom # 637: Communicate & Advocate For Your Online Learning... ask questions early & often - don't allow yourself to bury confusing content, unanswered questions, or misunderstandings... advocate for yourself, to be heard, to be understood, for clarity... the classroom needs you as much as you need it... so please be an active participant.

Communication is essential in all success... in education, business, friendships, relationships, family, team sports, gaming, in everything online and offline. For successful communication, it's important to fully understand the various communication forms at your disposal, and which method is most appropriate to effectively communicate your message.... written letters, emails, phone calls, texts, online messaging within apps, or face-to-face conversations... remember there's an appropriate time, place, and situation for each communication medium.

Beyond giving and receiving information, it's the vital collaborative and shared information which significantly enhances and strengthens learning, knowledge, and relational bonds within the online community. Here are two distinct communication strategies to incorporate in your daily learning journey.

Communicate & Advocate For Your Online Learning : Ask questions early & often... don't allow yourself to bury confusing content, unanswered questions, or misunderstandings... and don't allow yourself to get behind in studies and become frustrated. Communicate early and advocate for yourself, to be heard, to be understood, and for clarity... but certainly with appropriate tone & language, remembering to lead with kindness and positives, in all communication. Your teachers are ready & willing to offer

71

guidance… understand your teachers' preferred method of communication and use it well. The classroom needs you as much as you need it… so please be an active participant. Your experiences and contributions add value to the classroom and overall online learning community.

Collaborate & Challenge : You are never learning in isolation. There's a large network of like-minded peers and supportive educators within your learning community, waiting to work with you, to help you in every way possible… but it requires you, to reach out for help & assistance, and also be equally helpful to others. An easy way to start is by making a friend in each class, and deciding to challenge each other to collaborate daily about your online educational experience. Each day, share with each other something you learned, share an important assignment requirement, share an answer to a difficult question, or share any concerns or struggles you may have throughout the online process. Together, you support and uplift each other, you create your own "think tank" and your own knowledge center… to tap into whenever you need.

TELL ME   AND   I MAY FORGET

TEACH ME   AND   I MAY REMEMBER

INVOLVE ME AND   I WILL UNDERSTAND

PARTICIPATE, GET INVOLVED, CONQUER YOUR DREAMS !

EVERYTHING YOU DREAM OF LIVES INSIDE YOUR DAILY HABITS AND INSPIRED ROUTINES

No Joke Academic Axiom # 641: Some habits comfort us... other habits carve out the greatness in us - the key is to find comfort in habits of greatness ! ... Everything you dream of, lives inside your daily habits and inspired routines... literally everything !

Daily Habits & Inspired Routines : From the first day the world began, until the very end of time, some principles will remain etched in timeless truth... if nothing else, remember this one timeless truth : **We Are What We Repeatedly Do.**

There are no exceptions... success and failure are directly tied to our daily habits and routines. Some habits comfort us... sleeping in late is comforting, eating bad foods is comforting, binging on television and all night video-gaming is comforting, our mobile phones and social media addictions are comforting. But there is little growth in comfort, not nearly enough daily growth to achieve the great things you desire for your life.

Any and all success is driven by daily habits and routines, encompassing every aspect of our lives, whether its our health & fitness, our education & careers, our earnings & wealth, our goals & dreams...habits can make you or break you... in success, everything is connected to our habits.

Successful people practice successful habits everyday, not just occasionally... and they've been practicing these habits since childhood. Think about it... the greatest athletes have been practicing sports since childhood,... the greatest singers & musicians have been practicing music since childhood... the greatest business people, the best physicians, the top people in every field have been practicing success habits since early in their

73

childhood. Now remind yourself of what you're practicing for in your own future, **and let your daily habits be proof of that.**

Habits are daily routines and attitudes you engage without thinking… It's an attitude - so wake up everyday with an 'attitude' of accomplishments, an attitude of greatness !

> **"THE GREATEST DISCOVERY OF ALL TIME IS THAT
> A PERSON CAN CHANGE HIS FUTURE
> BY MERELY CHANGING HIS ATTITUDE."**
> - Oprah Winfrey

Everyday you wake up, remind yourself of everything you dream of…. if you dream of musical stardom, make it a daily habit to write incredible lyrics, a daily habit getting a little better playing that instrument, and remind yourself of your future rise in the music industry… if your dream of owning your own business, make it a daily habit to read about successful business startups, listen to CEO interviews from every business sector, and remind yourself of the incredible business empire you'll soon build… if you dream of one day being a world renowned doctor, make it a daily habit to devour information on the latest medical challenges and trends, and remind yourself that you're the future inventor of an amazing technology to cure millions of people around the world… everyday, when you wake up, the first thing you should do, as your feet hit the floor, is remind yourself of WHO you are and WHAT you're destined to achieve… then set in motion the daily habits to get you closer to those goals, each & every day. Everything you dream of, lives inside your daily habits and inspired routines… literally everything !

> **"THE MEANING OF THINGS LIES NOT IN THE THINGS THEMSELVES,
> BUT IN OUR ATTITUDE TOWARDS THEM."**
> - Antoine de Saint-Exupery

PUT IT ALL IN WRITING
BE INSPIRED & DRIVEN
BY YOUR OWN WORDS

No Joke Academic Axiom # 654 : Put It All In Writing ! ...writing down the daily details of your plan serves as a reminder and guide of what actually needs to be done... what, when, how, and why. When you put it all in writing, you begin to feel the energy pulling you to taking action... and ultimate execution.

Thinking about your goals and developing a daily plan is a first step to academic excellence... as they say, if you can dream it, you can achieve it. Yet, writing down the daily details of your plan is the critical next step toward taking action, serving as a reminder and constant guide of what actually needs to be done... what, when, how, and why. When you put it all in writing, you begin to feel the energy pulling you to taking action... and ultimate execution.

IF YOU FAIL TO PLAN,
THEN YOU'RE PLANNING TO FAIL !

Putting your plan into writing makes it easier to brainstorm, analyze, and adjust all the factors which make each day successful. Organizing your written plan helps you determine priorities, manage crucial deadlines, and avoid serious mistakes. Putting your plan in writing reduces the stress of having to remember everything, which frees your mental capacity to actually be more productive & creative. Everyday, write in your daily planner, take action toward your goals, track your progress and accomplishments, and make your dreams come alive. Put It All In Writing !

Top Strategies To Straight A's & Academic Excellence

DO NOW

1) No Joke Academic Axiom # 611: Distraction & procrastination are siblings of self-sabotage... don't sabotage yourself. Self discipline to avoid procrastination & distraction, is simply another way to show the world who you are, and what you're made of.

2) No Joke Academic Axiom # 623 : Create a workspace, inspired by your goals & dreams, and driven by the life you ultimately want to live... your workspace is where dreams are built, brick by brick, day by day... it can be anything you determine... but it must be inspirational if nothing at all.

3) No Joke Academic Axiom # 637: Communicate & Advocate For Your Online Learning... ask questions early & often - don't allow yourself to bury confusing content, unanswered questions, or misunderstandings... advocate for yourself, to be heard, to be understood, for clarity... the classroom needs you as much as you need it... so please be an active participant.

**4) No Joke Academic Axiom # 641: Some habits comfort us...
other habits carve out the greatness in us - the key is to find
comfort in habits of greatness ! ...** Everything you dream of,
lives inside your daily habits and inspired routines... literally
everything !

**5) No Joke Academic Axiom # 654 : Put It All In Writing ! -
writing down the daily details of your plan serves as a
reminder and guide of what actually needs to be done...** what,
when, how, and why. When you put it all in writing, you'll feel
the energy pulling you to taking action and ultimate execution.

BONUS

TOP THIRTY
AIN'T NO JOKE
Academic Axioms

&

FIVE STEPS TO
Quick Jumpstart
STRAIGHT-A'S

&

A PARTING
Memory
ALL THESE B'S !!

Top Thirty No Joke Academic Axioms
Straight A's & Academic Excellence

1 Accept The Straight-A Challenge

- You deserve academic excellence, accept it !

2 Give Yourself Credit

- Recognize the hard work you currently do
- Make small changes that lead to big results

3 Change Your Mindset

- Understand purpose & importance of 0 to 18
- Get serious & make the most of your teen years

4 Embrace The Urgency

- A childhood is a very short time to prepare for real life
- This is your time, your turn, take action now !

5 Treat The Classroom As Sacred

- Get maximum knowledge within the classroom
- Do not tolerate or accept distractions from friends

6 Understand Time & Place For Everything

- Focus on what's important at that moment
- Study when it's time to study, play when it's time to play

7 Build Your Personal Brand In The Classroom

- Your behavior and quality of work represents you
- Develop your work ethic, focus, and attention to detail
- Your brand matters to your image, company, & future

8 Draw The Line - Disrespecting Teachers

- Display upmost respect for teachers
- Respect the learning process & the giver of knowledge

9 Draw The Line - Skipping Class
- Show up everyday for your own future
- Make the classroom your safe space for learning & support

10 Daily Reading - the most important life building activity
- Improves Vocabulary & Expands Word Knowledge
- Develops Analytical Thinking Skills
- Improves Memory, Focus, and Concentration
- Enhances CREATIVITY & mental FLEXIBILITY.
- Reading gives your dreams the freedom to soar

11 Bookstore Reading Activity
- Circle around the bookstore, visit & scan books in each section
- Grab one that catches your eye, read the cover & back
- Skim tables of contents, find any section which interests you
- Then read just one page… get inspired !

12 No Nomophobia
- Just say No to Nomophobia - mobile phones addiction.
- Don't allow yourself to be controlled & manipulated
- Don't let your device control & program you
- Use phone settings, program your phone to respect your education

13 Develop Your Ability to Compete
- Challenge yourself to be a better person everyday…
- Compete in & out of the classroom
- Compete in every aspect of life, to bring out your very best.
- Anything someone else can do, so can you !

14 Class Participation
- Be an active & engaged learner…simple yet effective effort
- Increases retention of vital information
- Enhances engagement, understanding, clarity, and subject

15 100% On All Homework, Projects, & Extra Credit
- 100% on anything you are able to take home and complete…
- 100% complete, 100% correct, 100% on time, 100% of the time.

16 Study to learn and to understand, not to memorize.

- Knowledge is something nobody can ever take away from you.
- Memorization is short and fleeting...
- Education, knowledge and understanding, are forever.

17 Study Anywhere, Everywhere, Anytime.

- Keep book bag with you at all times, with all school materials
- Study every chance, everywhere you go, waste no idle time
- Be prepared and ready, to study anywhere, everywhere, anytime.

18 Set Daily Study Structure & Schedule

- Connect your daily activities with your goals and dreams...
- Understand your learning styles & how you learn best
- Set goals for each day
- Clear-out & clean-out a comfortable quiet home study zone...
- Treat this time as sacred, and chip away at your great future.

19 No Homework? - No Wasted Time

- Be productive with self improvement...
- No homework - read interesting self-help books & talk to mentor
- No homework - improve academic & content weaknesses
- No homework - research career / college / business interests
- No homework - develop writing skills, study foreign language, practice music instrument, improve video editing/programming skills, read for academic & personal growth, everyday.

20 Learn Alternatively

- Be a self-driven, self-guided, self-directed, self-taught guru.
- Be diligent, persistent, and tenacious, tirelessly chasing down resources that shed brighter light on the subject, class, topic materials. - ex. Khan Academy, Podcasts, Youtube, etc.

21 Intangibles - Diminish & Dismiss The Drama

- Practice Restorative Justice, conflict resolution, deescalation
- Maintain a calm learning environment
- No drama, no altercations, no suspensions, no missed school days

22 Intangibles - Collaborate With Like Minded Classmates
- Each class, make a friend - be a friend - keep a friend
- Collaborate effectively toward academic excellence.

23 Intangibles - Never Miss An Easy-A Opportunity.
- Resist the traps of not dressing out in P.E./Gym class, not rehearsing in Theatre, not painting in Art, not practicing an instrument in Music, not making a donut in home economics.
- For classes not academically demanding, bring energy & effort
- Easy-A classes leads to straight-A's

24 Intangibles - Student Grade App
- Utilize student grade apps daily
- Recognize you can't improve a thing, if you don't check a thing

25 Intangibles - Organized Personal Growth
- Set aside a block of time everyday for your homework studies.
- Improve weaknesses, plan your future, and working on personal growth…whether you're assigned homework or not.

26 Intangibles - Win The Day
- Approach straight-A's one day at a time & win each day….
- Quiet your mind, calm your heart, and do whatever is required of this day… WIN THE DAY !

27 Intangibles - No Sleeping On The Power of Daily Habits
- Your future is determined by what you repeatedly do everyday
- Simple positive daily habits can make you great
- Small negative habits can break you down

28 Draw The Line On Wasting Time
Time is the most expensive commodity ever, more valuable than gold, silver, diamonds, and all the money in the world… the clock is ticking - there's no backing up, no reverse, and no do-over - stop wasting time - change your life & change the world !!

29   Communicate & Advocate For Your Online Learning...

Ask questions early & often - don't allow yourself to bury confusing content, unanswered questions, or misunderstandings... advocate for yourself, to be heard, to be understood, for clarity... the classroom needs you as much as you need it... so please be an active participant.

30   Put It All In Writing !

Writing down the daily details of your plan serves as a reminder and guide of what actually needs to be done... what, when, how, and why. When you put it all in writing, you begin to feel the energy pulling you to taking action... and ultimate execution.

Quick Jumpstart Your Straight A's Journey
Five No Joke Academic Axioms

Implement, immediately, these five Quick Jumpstart No Joke Academic Axioms within your daily schedule, and observe significant grade improvements in 30 days or less.

1) Treat The Classroom As Sacred
- Learn as much as possible "inside" the classroom
- Do not tolerate or accept distractions from friends
- In the classroom, there's a major wealth transfer of knowledge & learning
- Many teachers teach & grade in small digestible chunks - savor the chunks
- Master the classroom, and you're 90% THERE !

2) Daily Study Structure Schedule
- Connect your daily activities with your goals and dreams
- Set goals for each day & be productive with self improvement
- No homework ? work on academic weaknesses & personal growth
- Clear-out & clean-out a comfortable quiet home study zone
- Treat this time as sacred, no nomophobia, and chip away at your great future.

3) Intangibles - Never Miss An Easy-A Opportunity.
- Many classes are not academically demanding, requires simple effort
- Resist the traps of not dressing out in P.E./Gym class, not rehearsing in Theatre, not painting in Art, not practicing an instrument in Music, not making a donut in Home Economics - it's just simple effort.
- Easy-A classes get you closer to straight-A report cards

4) 100% On All Homework, Projects, & Extra Credit
- 100% on anything assigned as take home and complete...
- 100% complete, 100% correct, 100% on time, 100% of the time.
- If you master the classroom from #1, then homework is easy & joyful !

5) Intangibles - Student Grade App
- Utilize student grade apps daily - this is a real game changer !
- Recognize "you can't improve a thing, if you don't check a thing !"
- Check Grade App **at least** 3x per day, before, during, and after school.

A Parting Memory : All These B's !!!

I guess if you really wanted to get to know me, to get an insight into my life's significant moments that shaped me into the person I am today, you could simply read this book's introduction at the beginning and then read my parting memory here at the end... both stories were critical to my pursuit of academic excellence and life-long learning.

In the introduction, I talked about my mother's announcement when I was in the 4th grade, of **"Don't bring no C's in my house!"** and pulling me off baseball team because I got one C on my report card in the 6th grade... well, at some point afterwards, she raised the bar further, in her normal fashion.

I'll always remember this scene from my junior year in high school, and to this day, I'm amazed at its impact on my psyche. As far back as I can remember, I was a good student, always at the top of my class, certainly due to the fact that my mother cared about education. She taught school, and she studied for her graduate degrees, and from the beginning of my life, education was the number one priority in our household. The word 'education' should have been written on our front door for the world to see. For our family, the relentless pursuit of education was our motto, our philosophy... it was "our thing". And at the earliest times in my childhood, my mother made it evident to me that education was an integral part of our existence... the expectations were clear & ever present, that we can & will exceed academically.

When I was in the 11th grade, I remember getting all 'B' grades in my English class for the first three terms of the year. One day, after a recent grading period, my mother walks into my room and unloads on me. I mean, she blessed me out... "B, B, B, what's going on with all these B's? You're not even trying, Keith. You know you're better than this."

She tightly gripped my report card in the palm of her hands, held high above her head, and shook it with fervor, as she said, "all these Beeezzzzz !!!"... and I swear I could see the sun flash a bright ray of light down on that report card as she shook it above her head, and suddenly a bunch of dark bold letter-B's starting popping off that paper like popcorn popping off a hot skillet... the more she shook it, the more those B's came popping off that paper and running around the room everywhere! I swear, I never seen so many B's in my life !

My initial thought was, "What the heck is she talking about? I mean, I did get a 'B', didn't I?" But like I've always done throughout my childhood, I took a quiet moment alone in my room to ponder my mother's words.

And the more I thought about it, the truth set in... that I was indeed just coasting... coasting on the many years of English and literature study in school and at home, coasting on the many books I'd read littered throughout our home, coasting on the piles of magazine subscriptions that I poured through, coasting on the many years of vocabulary and language workbooks in our home, coasting on the years of writing papers, reports & projects... coasting on a childhood orchestrated by a school-teaching-mother who taught me more at home than anything I've learned in a classroom. And in that moment, I knew she was right.

The expectations of my childhood, from my earliest memories, became present again. It was a familiar battle cry ... to discard the enemy of complacency. **I could do better, and to this day it amazes me that my mother knew that. I mean, she seemed so certain of it, so sure that I could do better... she spoke with a force of undeniable truth.** The truth is, that I had gotten bored. The English class was easy for me, my mind drifted, even during class, and the B's came without much effort. Somehow, my mother knew that.

Over the years, I've realized that parents have a sense of how talented their kids are, parents have a sense of the potential their children possess, and teachers have a sense of how good their students can be. As parents, raising children in this unforgiving world, we can no longer accept "good enough"... we've got to expect the full potential of our children to spring forth, and we've got to set expectations for it, uncompromisingly so.

I thank God everyday for saving me and blessing my life with an amazing woman who loved me dearly, a woman who raised me to accomplish all of my dreams... my mother, Evelyn Wright !

- Keith G. Wright, <u>AintNoJoke.com</u>

About The Author

Keith G. Wright is an award winning author for The Life Of Teenagers Ain't No Joke... Living A Courageous Childhood, In An Unforgiving World. Wright has built his career on motivating & inspiring youth to take a more serious look at their childhood, and live a courageous life through all obstacles... his list of titles have included :

Award Winning Author & Teen Mentor
Restorative Justice Coach & Practitioner
Assistant Principal - Adult & Community Education
GED Program Coordinator - Adult Education
MTSS Behavioral Coach
Community Involvement Specialist
Business Developer & Real Estate Investor

As a follow-up to his award winning motivational book, The Life Of Teenagers Ain't No Joke, Keith G. Wright has launched *Straight A's In Schools Ain't No Joke* to specifically help struggling students become excellent students.

Wright displays his talents to inspire youth to strive for their very best in his book, *Straight A's In Schools Ain't No Joke...* within these pages are key strategies and motivation to change your student's life. Simply, Keith G. Wright's *Straight A's In Schools*, moves middle & high school students, from the inactive into the inspired, and from the unwilling into the unstoppable !